EASY GUITAR

Taylor Swift

ISBN 978-1-4234-8162-1

HAL•LEONARD®
CORPORATION

7777 W. BLUEMOUND RD. P.O. BOX 13819 MILWAUKEE, WI 53213

Visit Hal Leonard Online at
www.halleonard.com

4 STRUM AND PICK PATTERNS

8 Tim McGraw

12 Picture to Burn

16 Teardrops on My Guitar

20 A Place in This World

24 Cold as You

5 The Outside

44 Tied Together with a Smile

28 Stay Beautiful

32 Should've Said No

36 Mary's Song (Oh My My My)

40 Our Song

STRUM AND PICK PATTERNS

This chart contains the suggested strum and pick patterns that are referred to by number at the beginning of each song in this book. The symbols ⊓ and ∨ in the strum patterns refer to down and up strokes, respectively. The letters in the pick patterns indicate which right-hand fingers plays which strings.

p = thumb
i = index finger
m = middle finger
a = ring finger

For example; Pick Pattern 2
is played: thumb - index - middle - ring

Strum Patterns

Pick Patterns

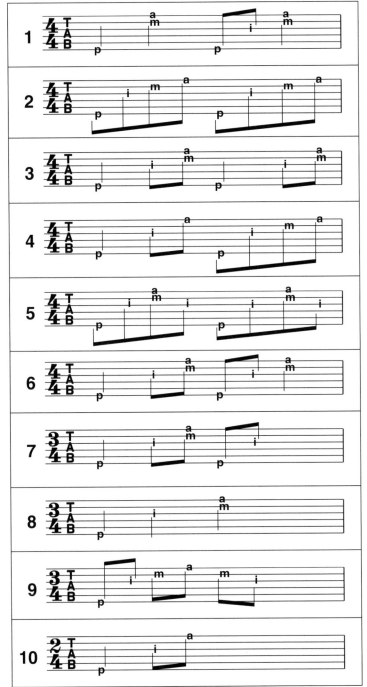

You can use the 3/4 Strum or Pick Patterns in songs written in compound meter (6/8, 9/8, 12/8, etc.). For example, you can accompany a song in 6/8 by playing the 3/4 pattern twice in each measure. The 4/4 Strum and Pick Patterns can be used for songs written in cut time (¢) by doubling the note time values in the patterns. Each pattern would therefore last two measures in cut time.

The Outside

Words and Music by Taylor Swift

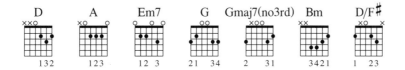

*Capo III

Strum Pattern: 3, 4
Pick Pattern: 4, 6

Intro
Moderately fast

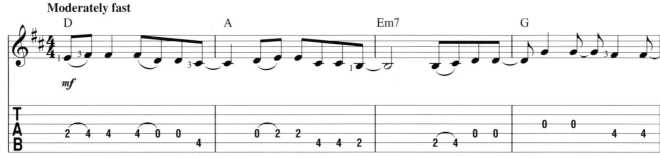

*Optional: To match recording, place capo at 3rd fret.

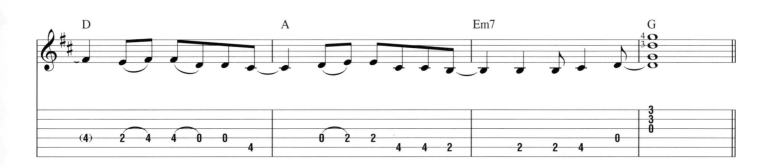

Verse

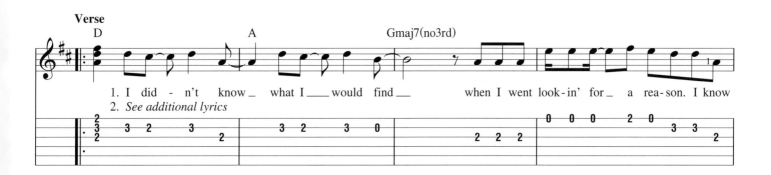

1. I did-n't know_ what I_ would find_ when I went look-in' for_ a rea-son. I know
2. *See additional lyrics*

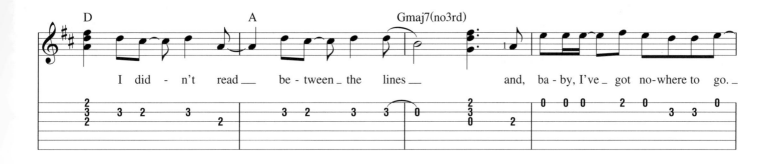

I did-n't read_ be-tween_ the lines_ and, ba-by, I've_ got no-where to go._

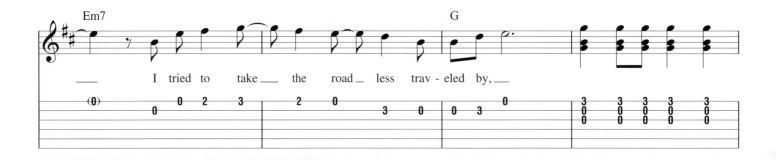

I tried to take __ the road __ less trav - eled by, __

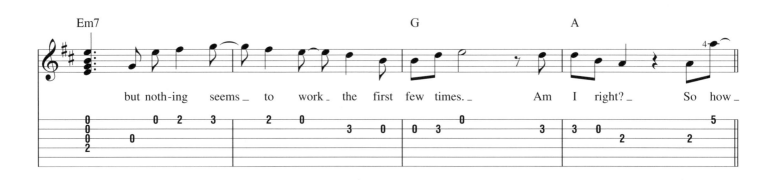

but noth-ing seems __ to work __ the first few times. __ Am I right? __ So how

𝄋 Chorus

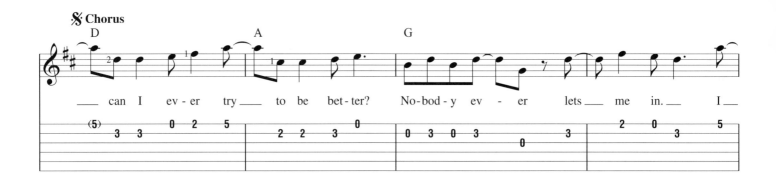

__ can I ev - er try __ to be bet - ter? No-bod - y ev - er lets __ me in. __ I

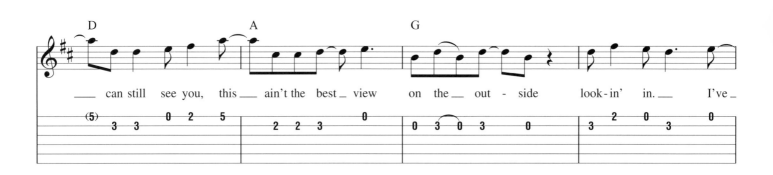

__ can still see you, this __ ain't the best __ view on the __ out - side look-in' in. __ I've

To Coda ⊕

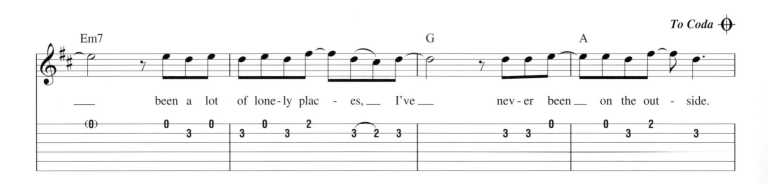

__ been a lot of lone - ly plac - es, __ I've __ nev - er been __ on the out - side.

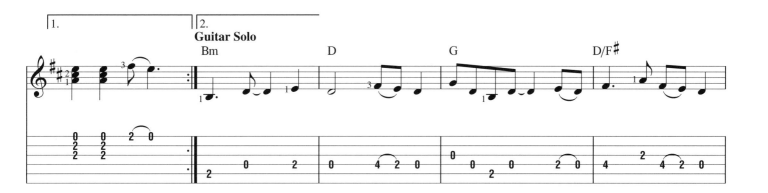

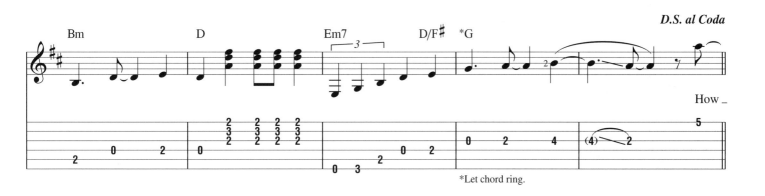

*Let chord ring.

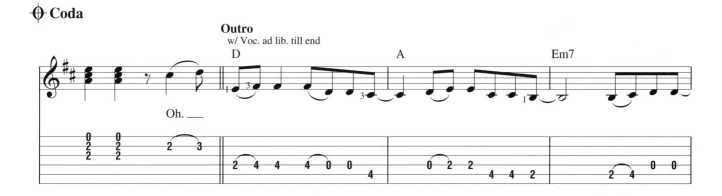

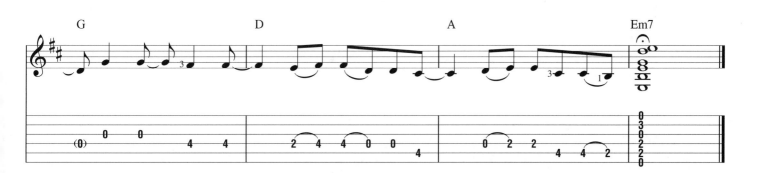

Additional Lyrics

2. You saw me there, but never knew
   That I would give it all up to be
   A part of this, a part of you.
   And now it's all too late. So, you see
   You could've helped if you had wanted to,
   But no one notices until it's too late to do anything.

Tim McGraw

Words and Music by Taylor Swift and Liz Rose

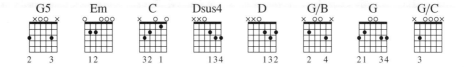

*Capo V

Strum Pattern: 3, 5
Pick Pattern: 1, 3

Intro

Moderately slow, in 2

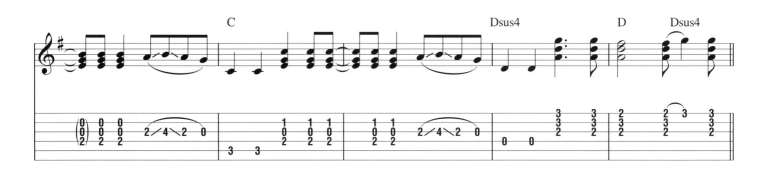

*Optional: To match recording, place capo at 5th fret.

Verse

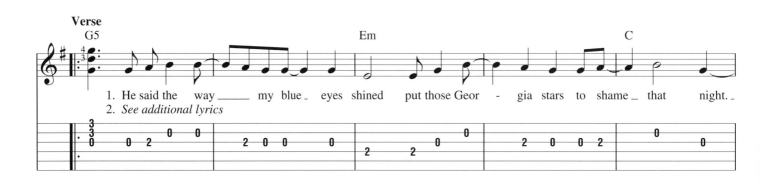

1. He said the way _____ my blue _ eyes shined put those Geor - gia stars to shame _ that night.
2. *See additional lyrics*

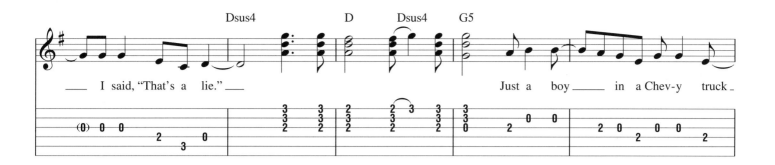

I said, "That's a lie." ___ Just a boy ___ in a Chev-y truck ___

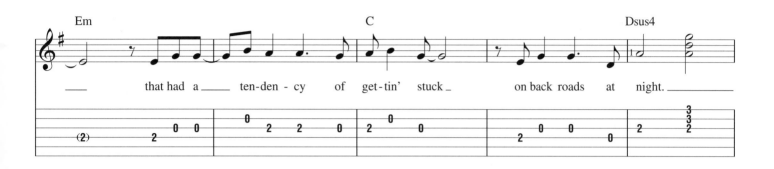

___ that had a ___ ten-den-cy of get-tin' stuck ___ on back roads at night. ___

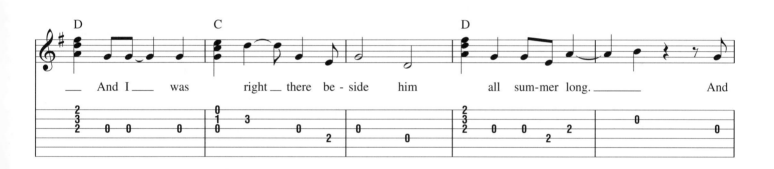

___ And I ___ was right ___ there be-side him all sum-mer long. ___ And

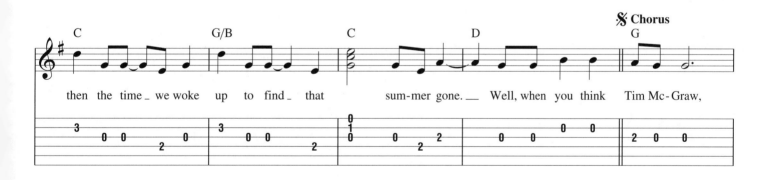

then the time ___ we woke up to find ___ that sum-mer gone. ___ Well, when you think Tim Mc-Graw,

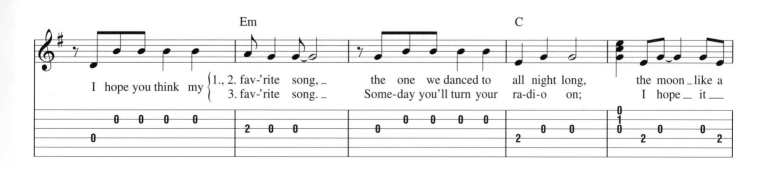

I hope you think my { 1., 2. fav-'rite song, ___ the one we danced to all night long, the moon ___ like a
                      3. fav-'rite song. ___ Some-day you'll turn your ra-di-o on; I hope ___ it ___

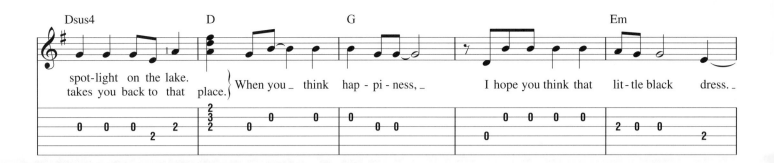

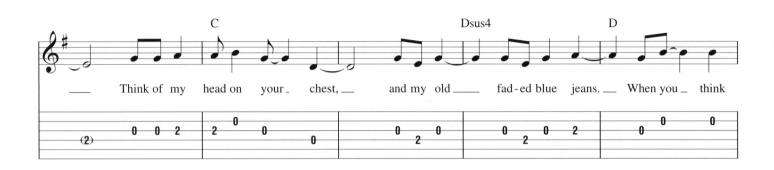

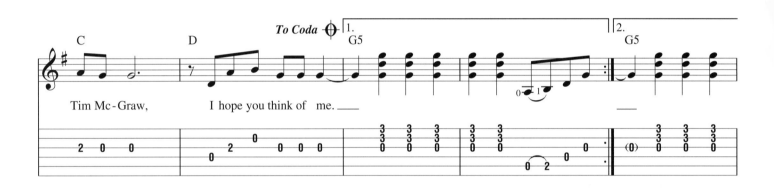

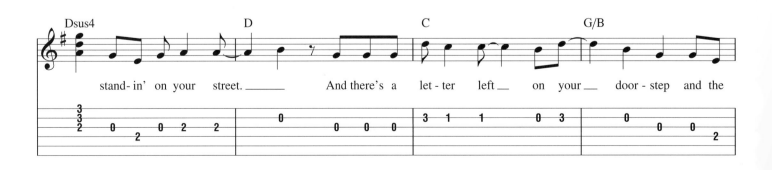

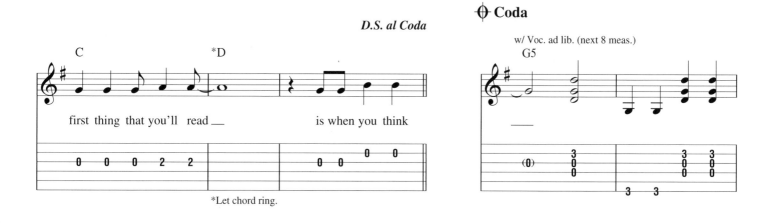

*Let chord ring.

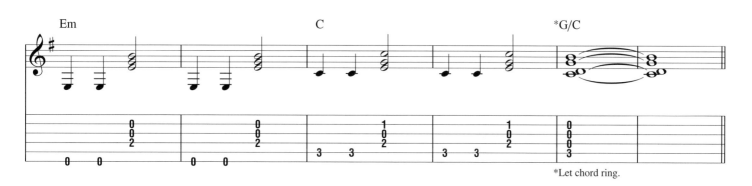

*Let chord ring.

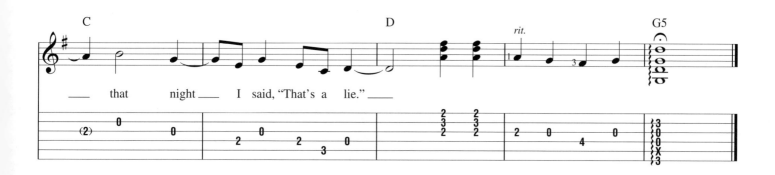

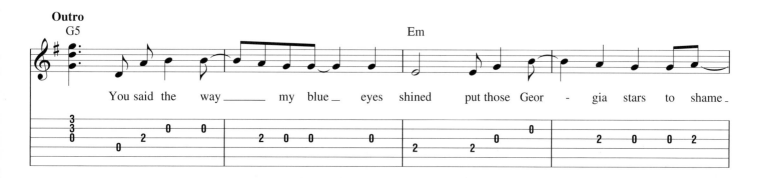

Additional Lyrics

2. September saw a month of tears,
   And thankin' God that you weren't here
   To see me like that.
   But in a box beneath my bed
   Is a letter that you never read
   From three summers back.
   It's hard not to find it all a little bittersweet.
   And lookin' back on all of that
   It's nice to believe when you think...

Picture to Burn

Words and Music by Taylor Swift and Liz Rose

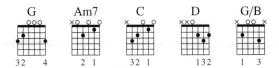

*Strum Pattern: 3, 4
*Pick Pattern: 4, 6

*Use Pattern 10 for 2/4 measures.

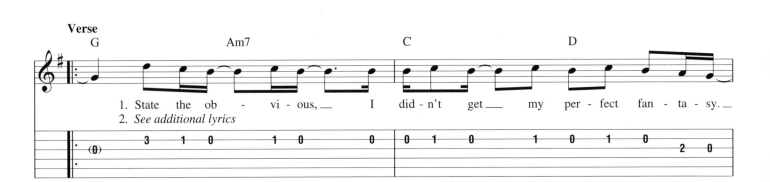

1. State the ob - vi - ous, __ I did - n't get __ my per - fect fan - ta - sy. __
2. *See additional lyrics*

__ I re - al - ize __ you love your - self more than you could ev - er love me. __

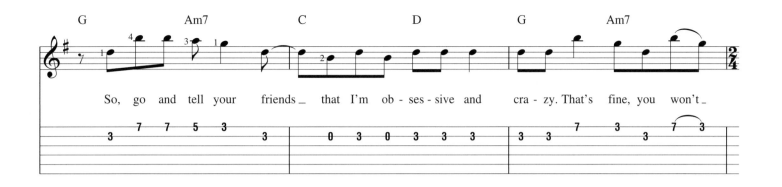

So, go and tell your friends _ that I'm ob - ses - sive and cra - zy. That's fine, you won't _

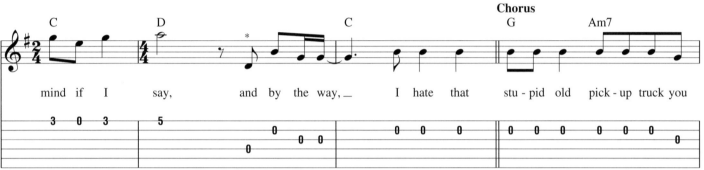

mind if I say, and by the way, _ I hate that stu - pid old pick - up truck you

*Sung one octave higher throughout chorus.

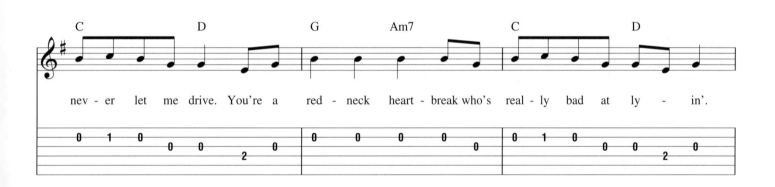

nev - er let me drive. You're a red - neck heart - break who's real - ly bad at ly - in'.

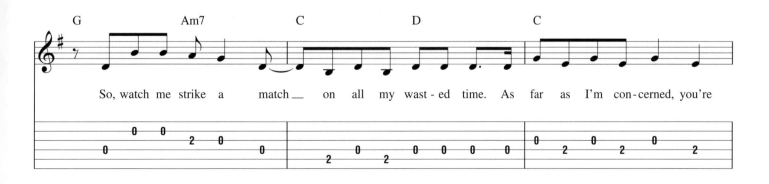

So, watch me strike a match _ on all my wast - ed time. As far as I'm con - cerned, you're

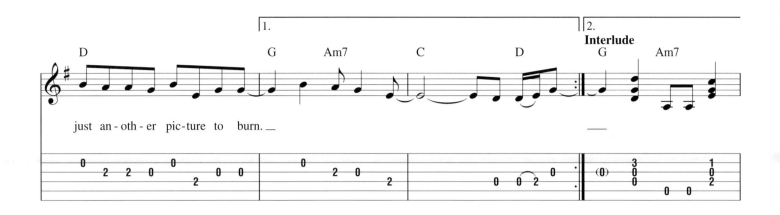

just an-oth-er pic-ture to burn. _

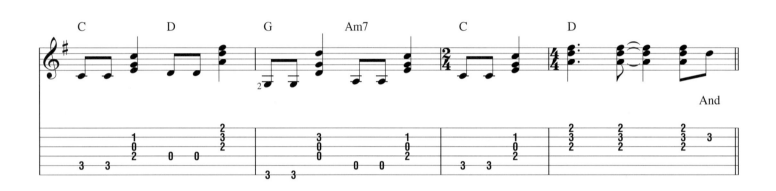

And

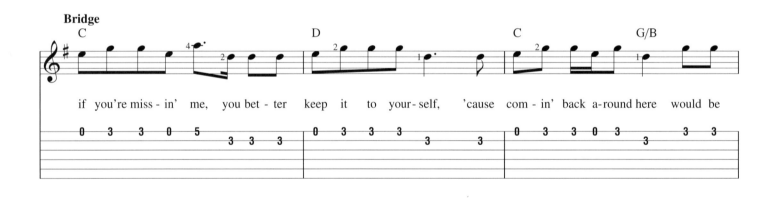

if you're miss-in' me, you bet-ter keep it to your-self, 'cause com-in' back a-round here would be

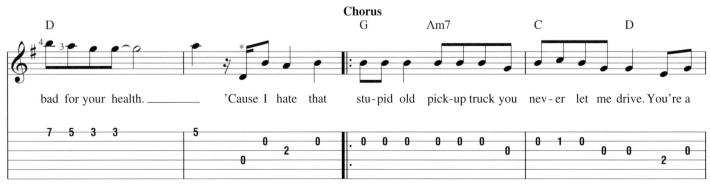

bad for your health. _____ 'Cause I hate that stu-pid old pick-up truck you nev-er let me drive. You're a

*Sung one octave higher throughout Chorus.

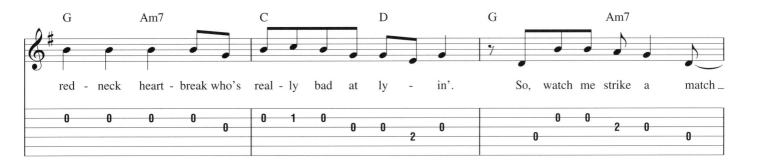

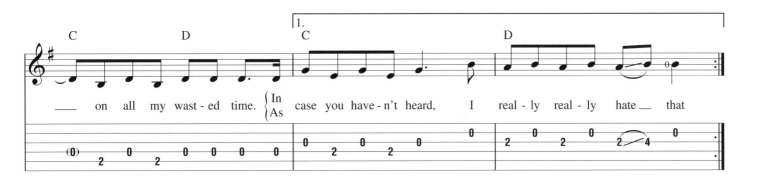

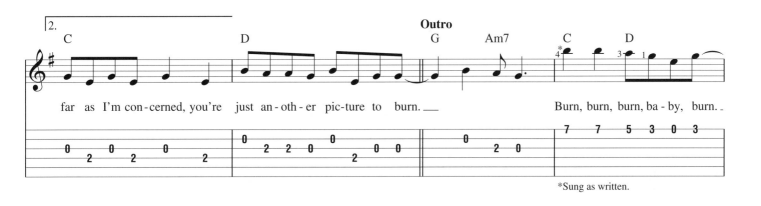

*Sung as written.

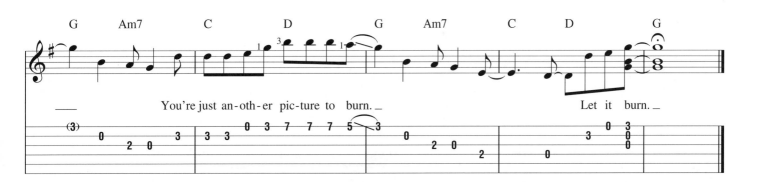

Additional Lyrics

2. There's no time for tears,
I'm just sittin' here plannin' my revenge.
There's nothin' stoppin' me,
I'm going out with all of your best friends.
And if you come around sayin' "sorry" to me,
My daddy's gonna show you how sorry you'll be.
'Cause I hate that...

Teardrops on My Guitar

Words and Music by Taylor Swift and Liz Rose

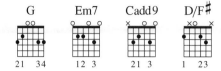

*Capo III

Strum Pattern: 3, 6
Pick Pattern: 2, 5

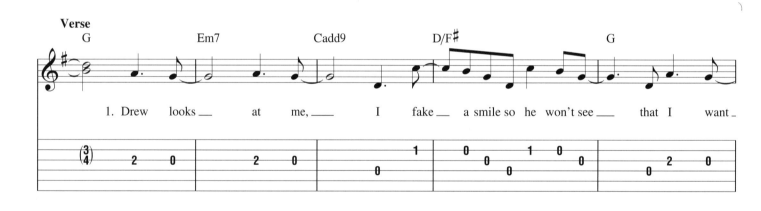

*Optional: To match recording, place capo at 3rd fret.

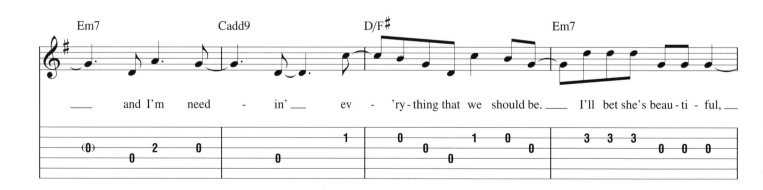

1. Drew looks ___ at me, ___ I fake ___ a smile so he won't see ___ that I want ___

___ and I'm need - in' ___ ev - 'ry-thing that we should be. ___ I'll bet she's beau - ti - ful,

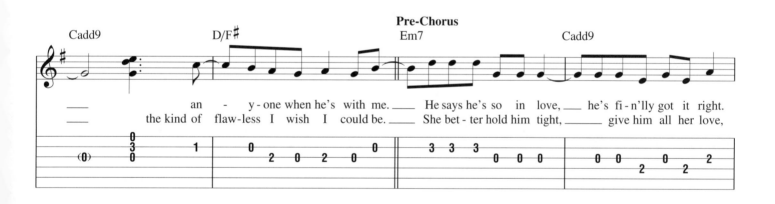

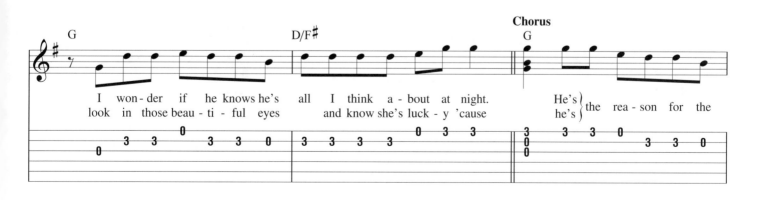

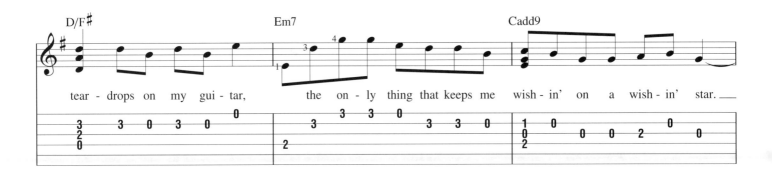

tear - drops on my gui - tar, the on - ly thing that keeps me wish - in' on a wish - in' star. ___

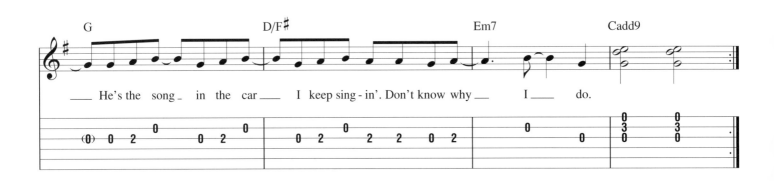

___ He's the song ___ in the car ___ I keep sing - in'. Don't know why ___ I ___ do.

Interlude

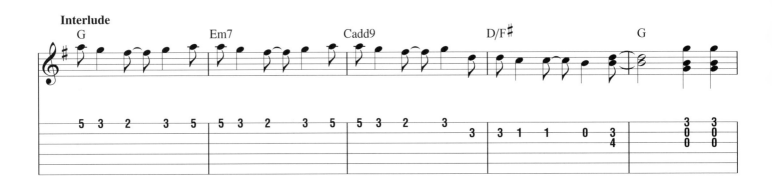

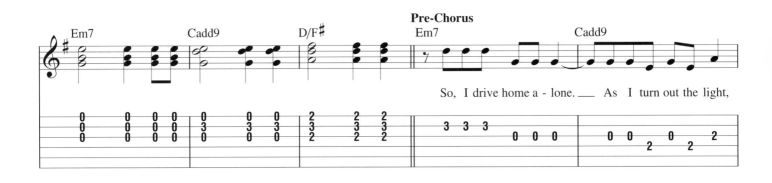

So, I drive home a - lone. ___ As I turn out the light,

Pre-Chorus

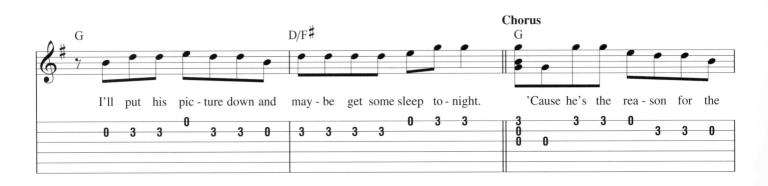

I'll put his pic - ture down and may - be get some sleep to - night. 'Cause he's the rea - son for the

Chorus

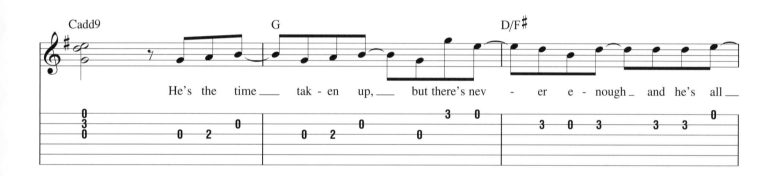

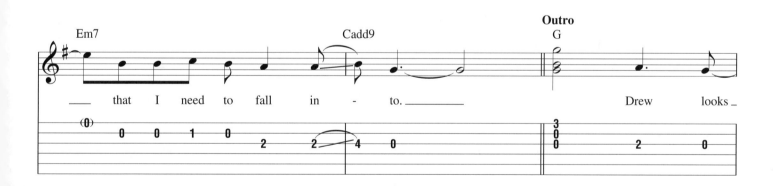

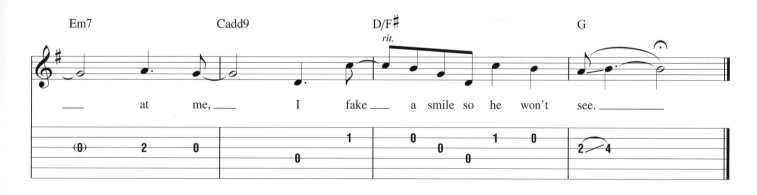

A Place in This World

Words and Music by Taylor Swift, Robert Ellis Orrall and Angelo

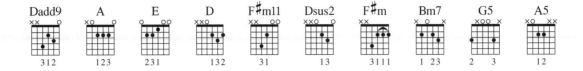

Strum Pattern: 4, 6
Pick Pattern: 4, 5

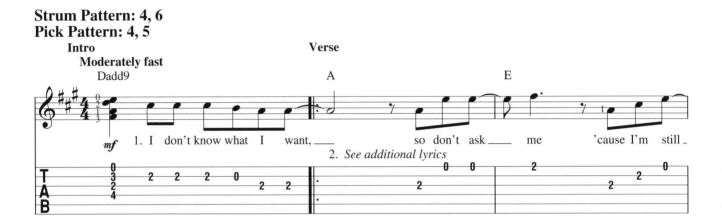

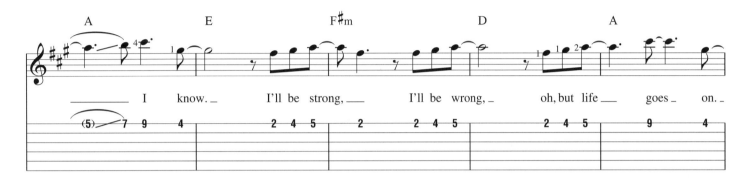

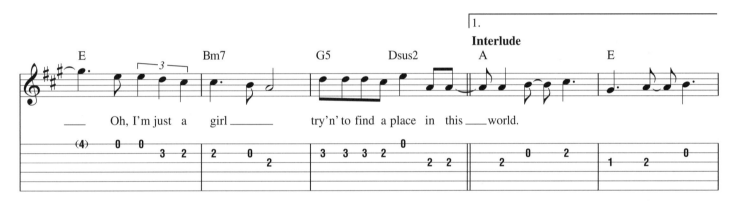

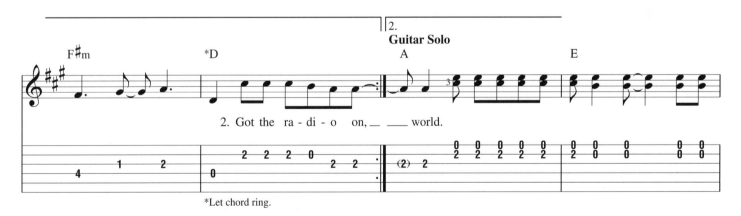

*Let chord ring.

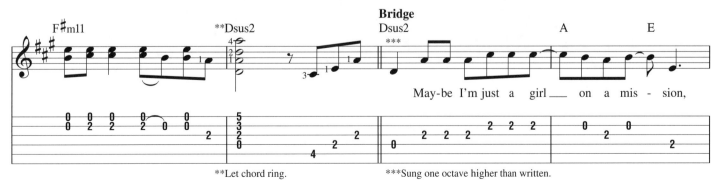

**Let chord ring.   ***Sung one octave higher than written.

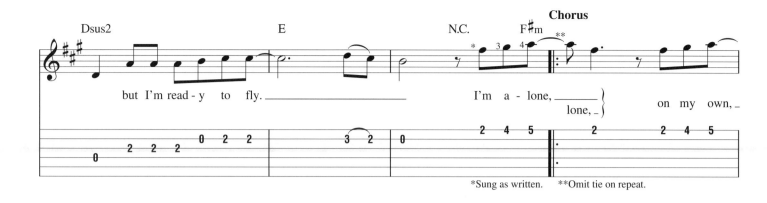

but I'm read-y to fly. _____ I'm a-lone, _____ on my own, ___
lone, ___

*Sung as written. **Omit tie on repeat.*

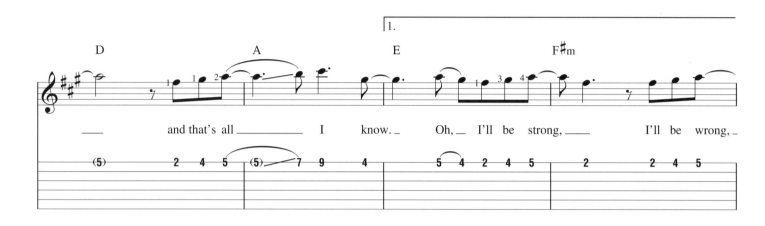

___ and that's all _____ I know. ___ Oh, ___ I'll be strong, _____ I'll be wrong, ___

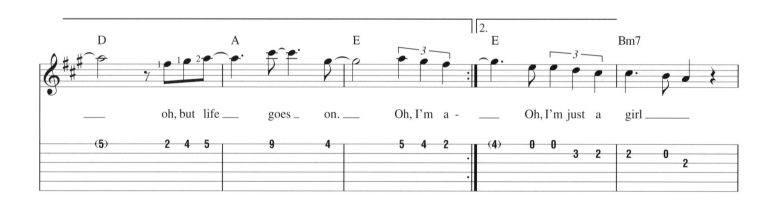

___ oh, but life ___ goes ___ on. ___ Oh, I'm a- ___ Oh, I'm just a girl ___

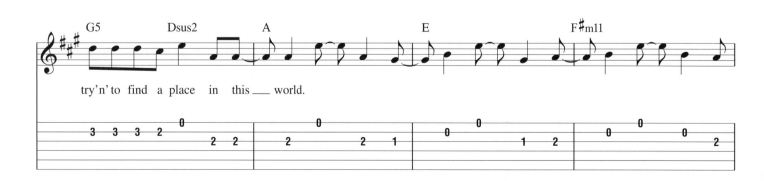

try'n' to find a place in this ___ world.

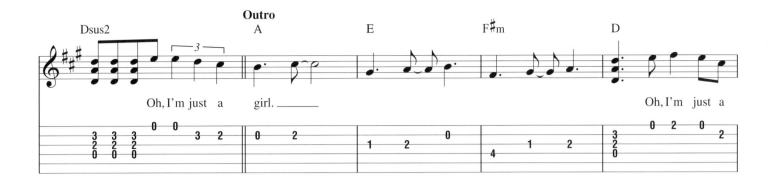

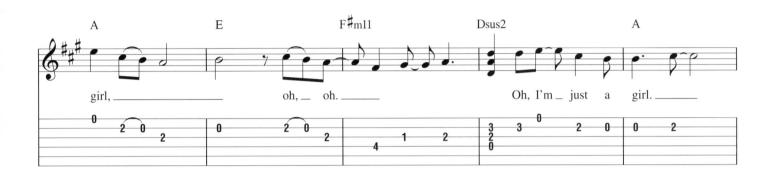

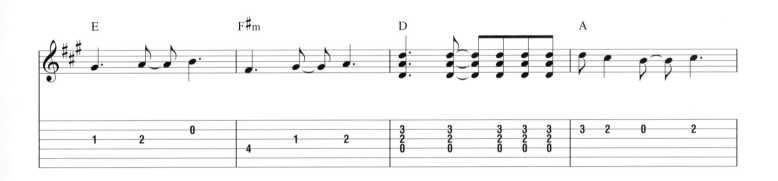

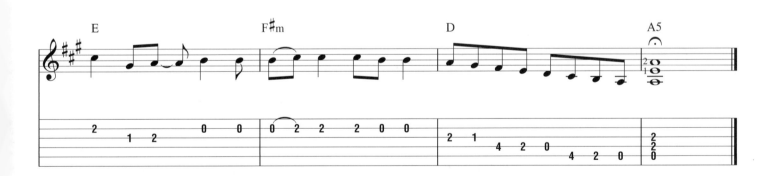

Additional Lyrics

2. Got the radio on, my old blue jeans,
   And I'm wearin' my heart on my sleeve.
   Feelin' lucky today, got the sunshine.
   Could you tell me what more do I need?
   And tomorrow's just a mystery, oh, yeah,
   But that's OK.

Cold as You

Words and Music by Taylor Swift and Liz Rose

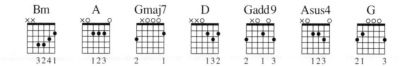

Bm   A   Gmaj7   D   Gadd9   Asus4   G

*Capo III

Strum Pattern: 3, 6
Pick Pattern: 2, 5

Intro
Moderately

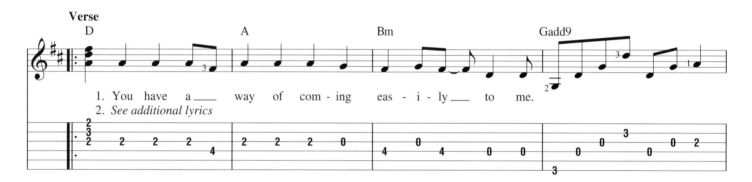

*Optional: To match recording, place capo at 3rd fret.

Verse

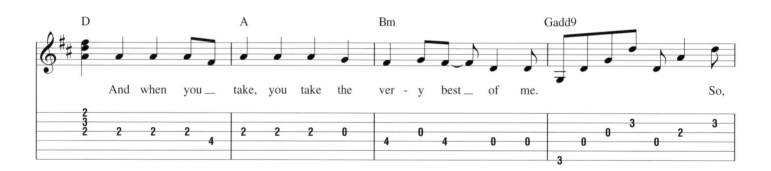

1. You have a ___ way of com-ing eas-i-ly ___ to me.
2. *See additional lyrics*

And when you ___ take, you take the ver-y best ___ of me. So,

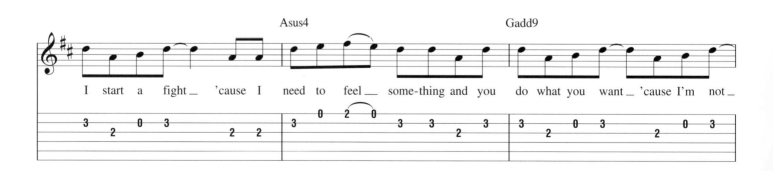

I start a fight ___ 'cause I need to feel ___ some-thing and you do what you want ___ 'cause I'm not ___

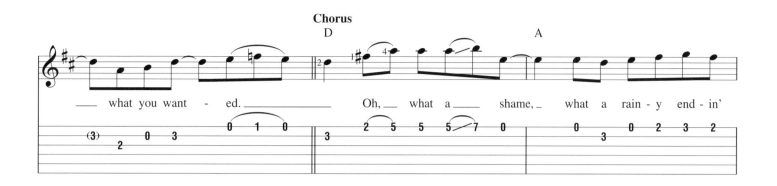

Chorus

_____ what you want - ed. _____ Oh, _____ what a _____ shame, _____ what a rain - y end - in'

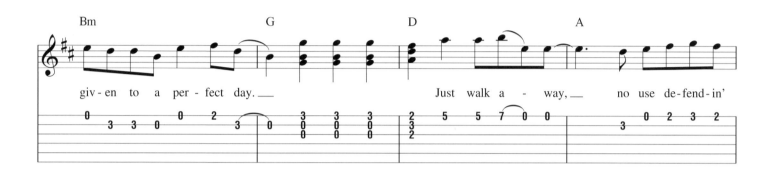

giv - en to a per - fect day. _____ Just walk a - way, _____ no use de - fend - in'

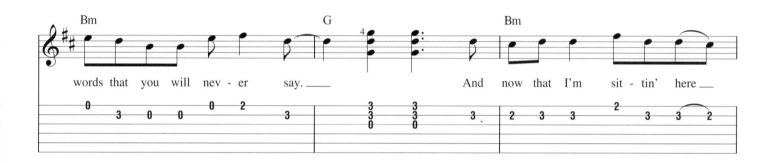

words that you will nev - er say. _____ And now that I'm sit - tin' here _____

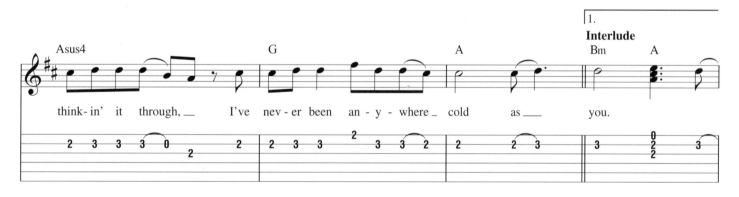

Interlude

think - in' it through, _____ I've nev - er been an - y - where _____ cold as _____ you.

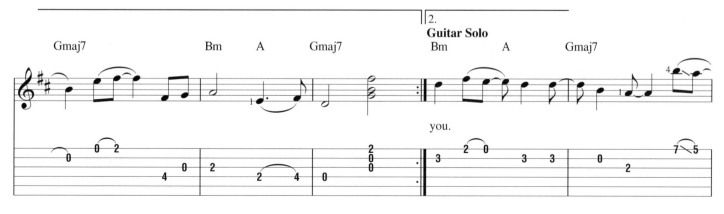

Guitar Solo

you.

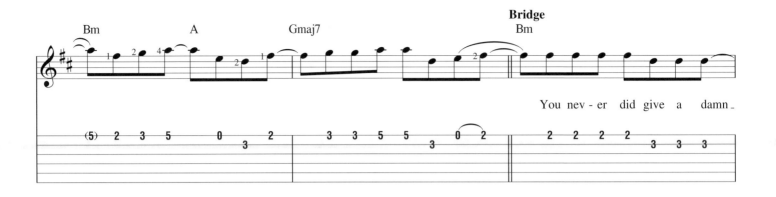

You nev-er did give a damn

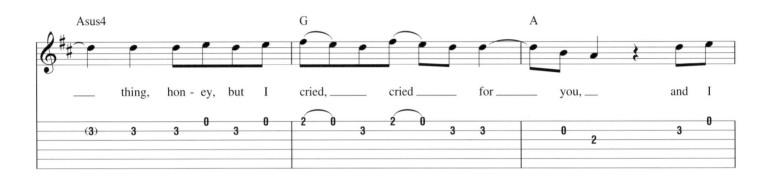

___ thing, hon-ey, but I cried, ___ cried ___ for ___ you, ___ and I

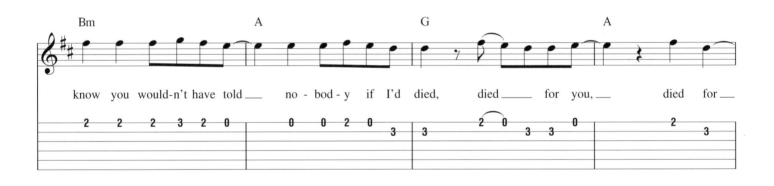

know you would-n't have told ___ no-bod-y if I'd died, died ___ for you, ___ died for

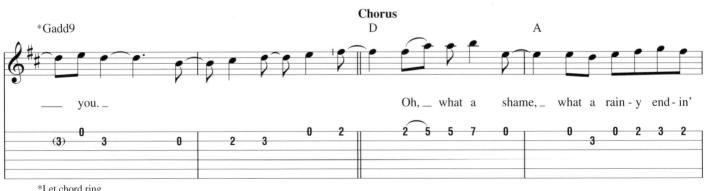

___ you. ___   Oh, _ what a shame, _ what a rain-y end-in'

*Let chord ring.

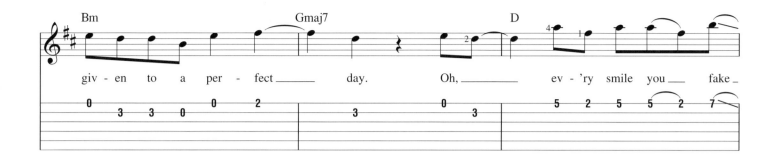

giv - en to a per - fect _____ day. Oh, _____ ev - 'ry smile you ___ fake _

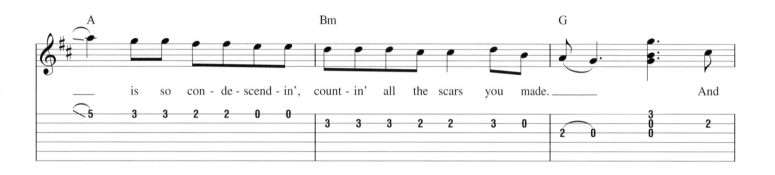

_____ is so con - de - scend - in', count - in' all the scars you made. _____ And

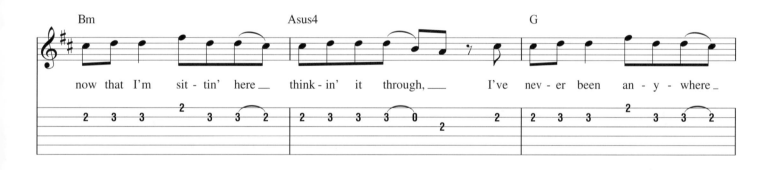

now that I'm sit - tin' here ___ think - in' it through, _____ I've nev - er been an - y - where _

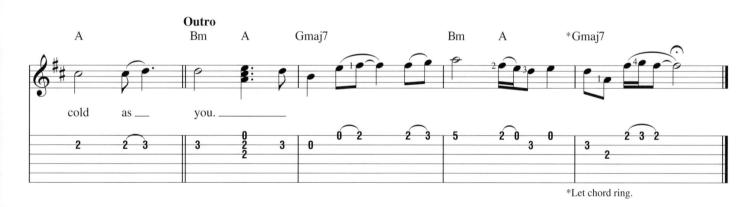

cold as ___ you. _____

*Let chord ring.

Additional Lyrics

2. You put up walls and paint them all a shade of gray.
   And I stood there lovin' you and wished them all away.
   And you come away with a great little story
   Of a mess of a dreamer with the nerve to adore you.

Stay Beautiful

Words and Music by Taylor Swift and Liz Rose

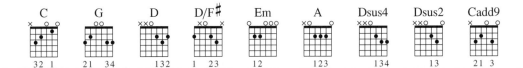

*Capo I

Strum Pattern: 4
Pick Pattern: 4

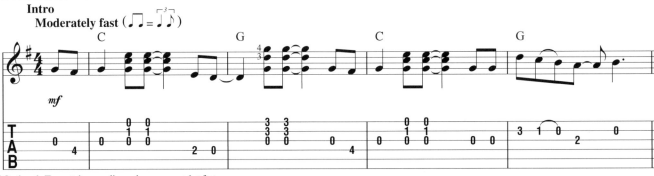

*Optional: To match recording, place capo at 1st fret

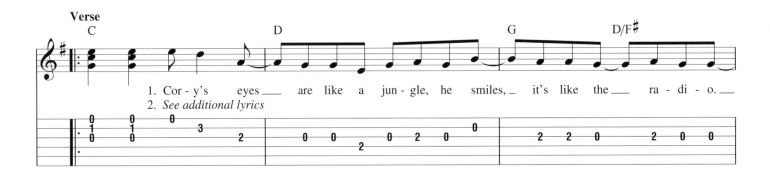

1. Cor - y's eyes ___ are like a jun - gle, he smiles, _ it's like the ___ ra - di - o. ___
2. *See additional lyrics*

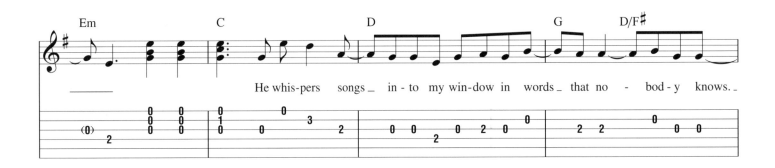

He whis - pers songs _ in - to my win - dow in words _ that no - bod - y knows.

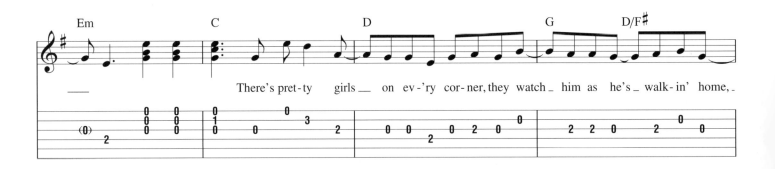

There's pret - ty girls ___ on ev - 'ry cor - ner, they watch _ him as he's _ walk - in' home,

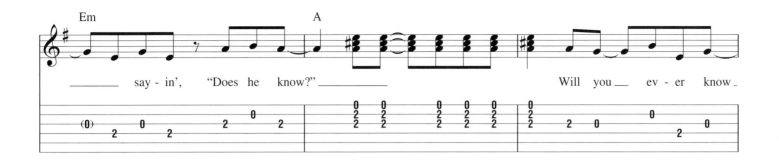

_____ say- in', "Does he know?" _____ Will you _ ev- er know _

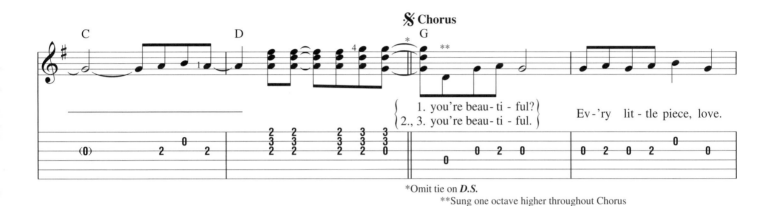

% **Chorus**

{ 1. you're beau-ti-ful? }
{ 2., 3. you're beau-ti-ful. }   Ev-'ry lit-tle piece, love.

*Omit tie on **D.S.**
**Sung one octave higher throughout Chorus

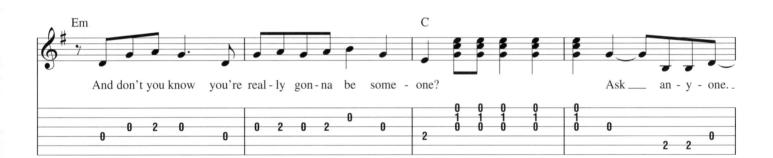

And don't you know you're real-ly gon-na be some-one?   Ask _ an-y-one. _

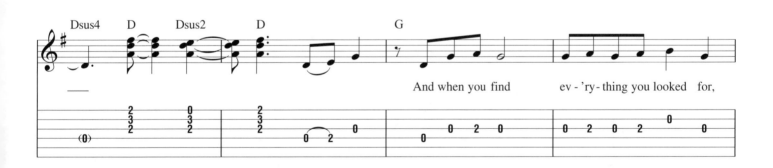

_ And when you find ev-'ry-thing you looked for,

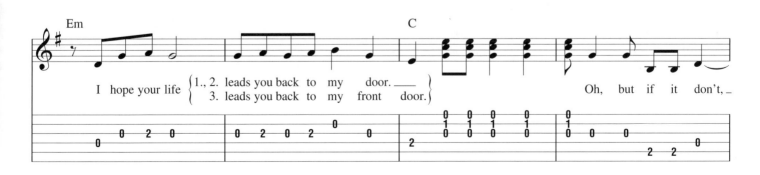

I hope your life { 1., 2. leads you back to my door. ___ }
{ 3. leads you back to my front door. }   Oh, but if it don't, _

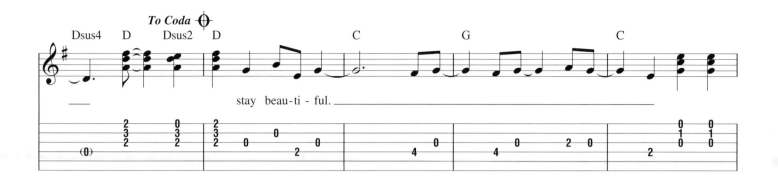

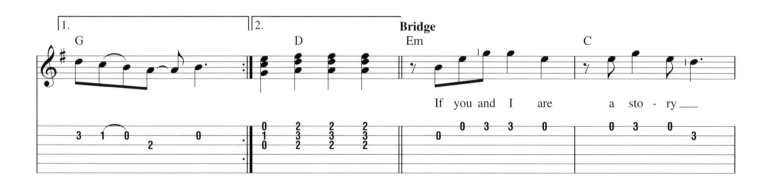

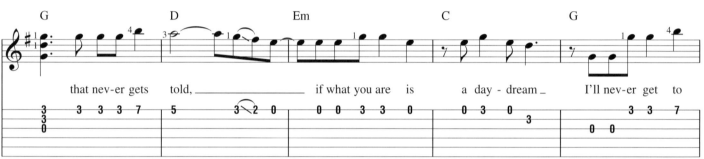

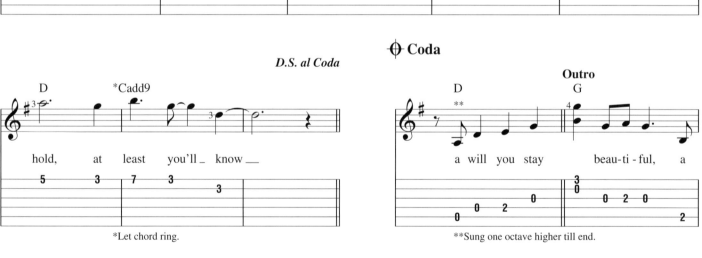

*Let chord ring.

**Sung one octave higher till end.

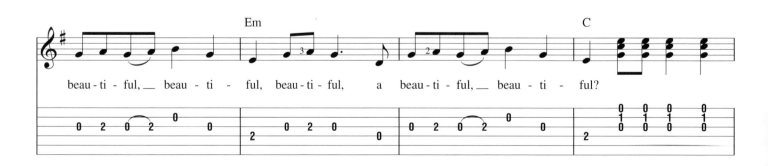

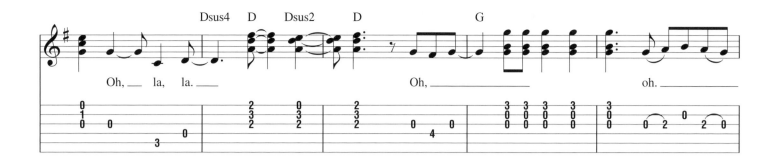

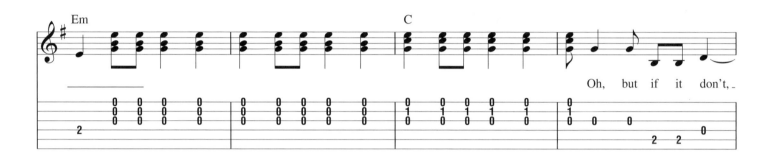

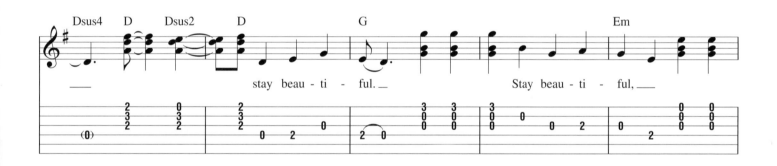

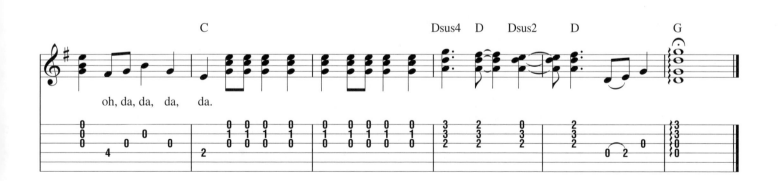

Additional Lyrics

2. Cory finds another way to be the highlight of my day.
I'm takin' pictures in my mind so I can save 'em for a rainy day.
It's hard to make conversation when he's takin' my breath away.
I should say, "Hey, by the way, you're beautiful."

Should've Said No

Words and Music by Taylor Swift

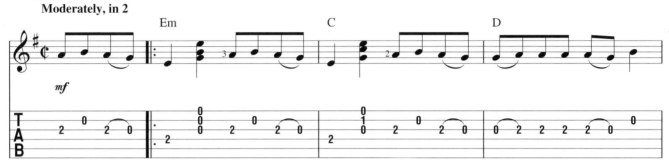

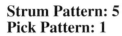
Strum Pattern: 5
Pick Pattern: 1

Intro
Moderately, in 2

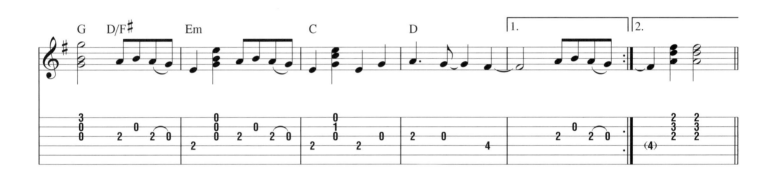

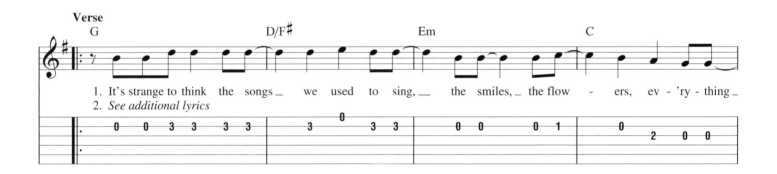

Verse

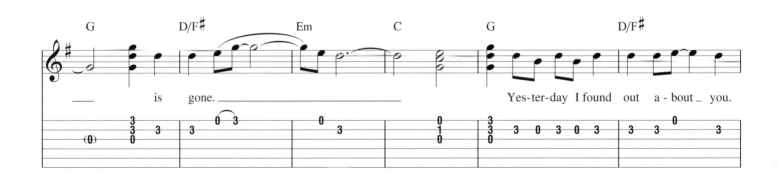

1. It's strange to think the songs _ we used to sing, _ the smiles, _ the flow - ers, ev - 'ry - thing _
2. *See additional lyrics*

_ is gone. _____ Yes-ter-day I found out a-bout _ you.

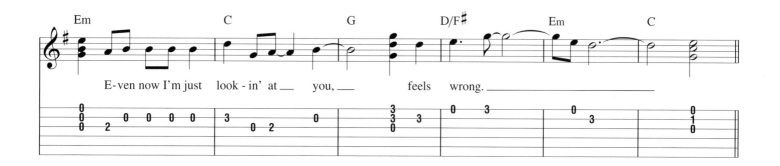

Pre-Chorus

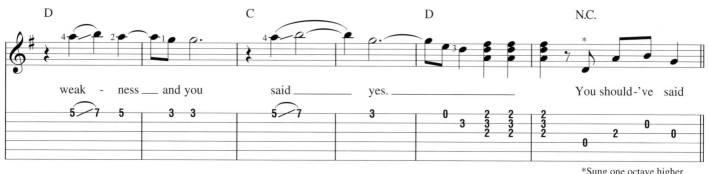

*Sung one octave higher throughout Chorus.

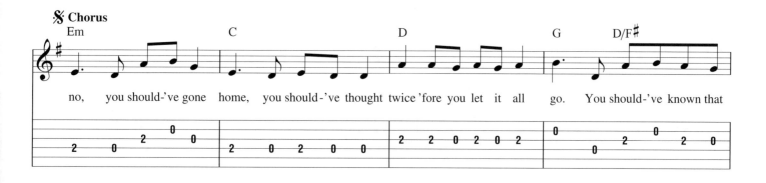

Chorus

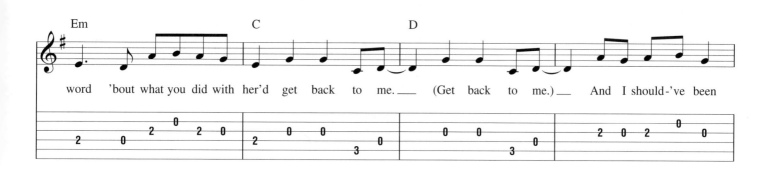

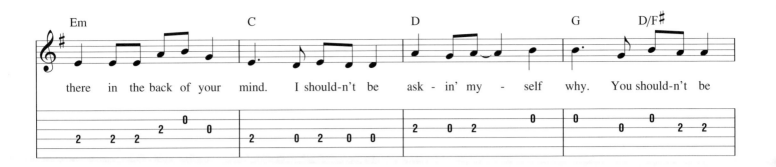

there in the back of your mind. I should-n't be ask - in' my - self why. You should-n't be

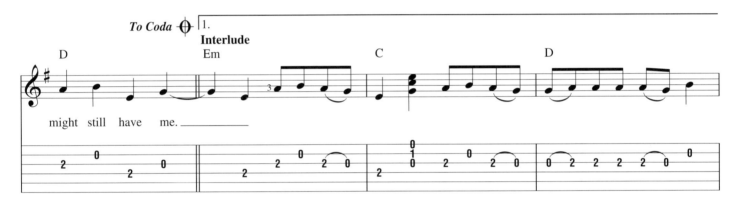

beg - gin' for __ for-give - ness at my feet. ___ You should-'ve said no, bab- by, and you

To Coda ⊕ │1.
Interlude

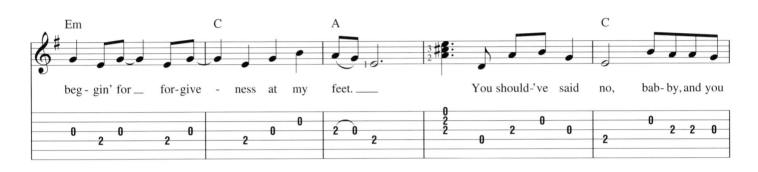

might still have me. _____

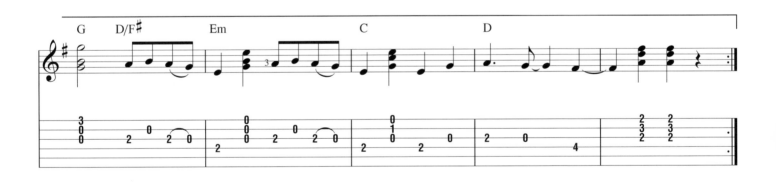

│2.
Guitar Solo

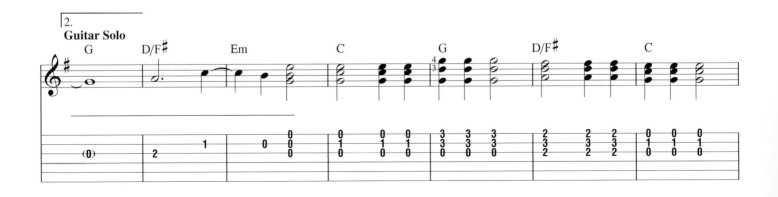

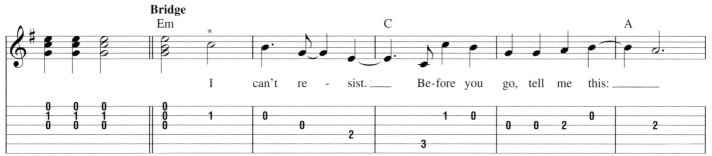

*Sung one octave higher throughout Bridge.

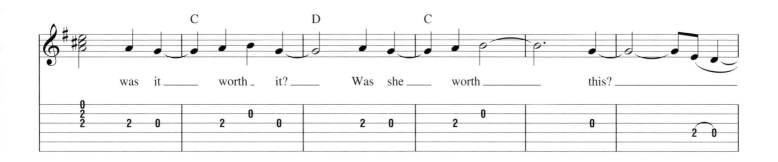

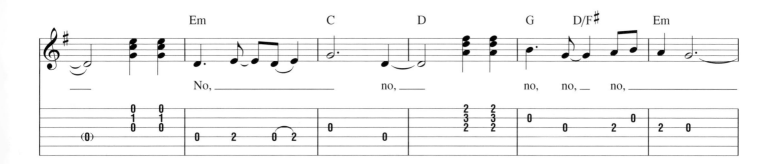

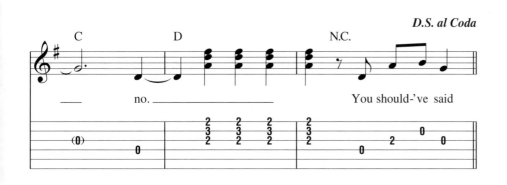

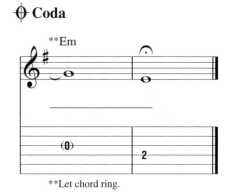

**Let chord ring.

Additional Lyrics

2. You can see that I've been cryin',
Baby, you know all the right things to say.
But do you honestly expect me to believe
We could ever be the same?

Mary's Song
(Oh My My My)

Words and Music by Taylor Swift, Liz Rose and Brian Maher

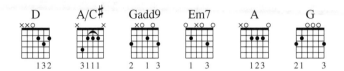

Strum Pattern: 3, 6
Pick Pattern: 2, 5

Intro
Moderately slow, in 2

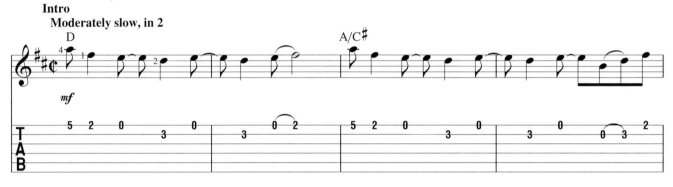

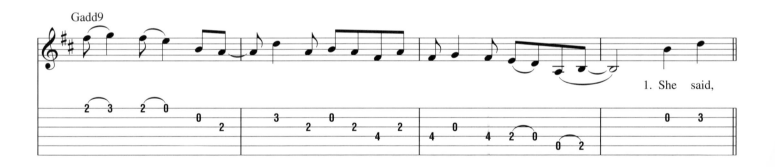

1. She said,

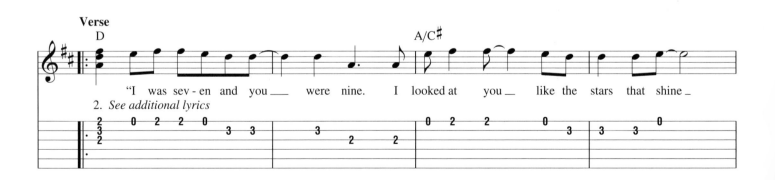

"I was sev-en and you ___ were nine. I looked at you ___ like the stars that shine ___

2. *See additional lyrics*

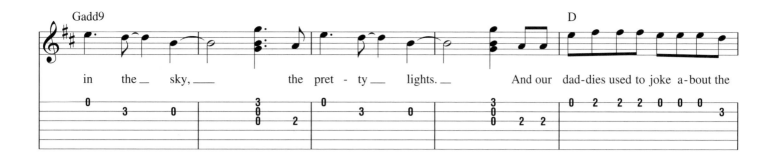

in the ___ sky, ___ the pret - ty ___ lights. ___ And our dad-dies used to joke a-bout the

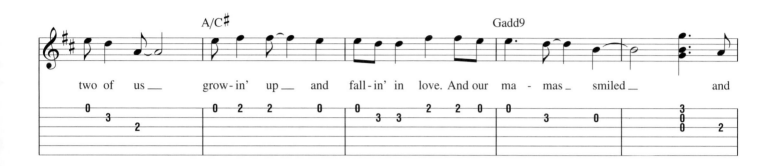

two of us ___ grow-in' up ___ and fall-in' in love. And our ma - mas ___ smiled ___ and

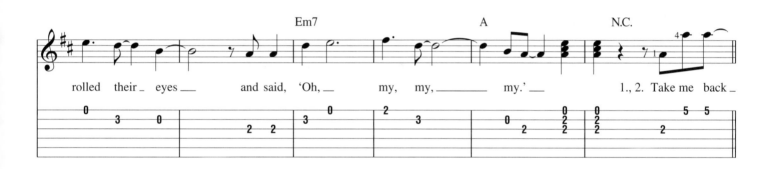

rolled their ___ eyes ___ and said, 'Oh, ___ my, my, ___ my.' ___ 1., 2. Take me back ___

𝄋 Chorus

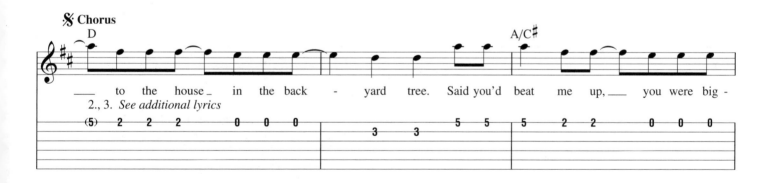

___ to the house ___ in the back - yard tree. Said you'd beat me up, ___ you were big -
2., 3. See additional lyrics

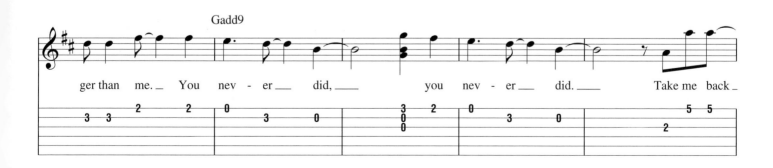

ger than me. ___ You nev - er ___ did, ___ you nev - er ___ did. ___ Take me back ___

37

when our world ___ was one ___ block wide. I dared ___ you to kiss ___ me and ran ___ when you tried. ___

To Coda ⊕

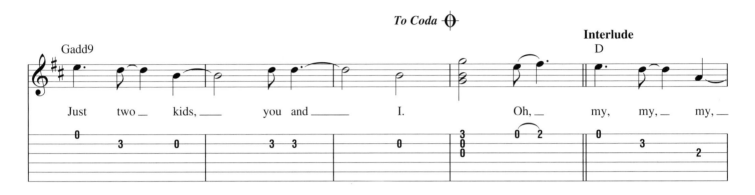

Just two ___ kids, ___ you and ___ I. Oh, ___ my, my, ___ my, ___

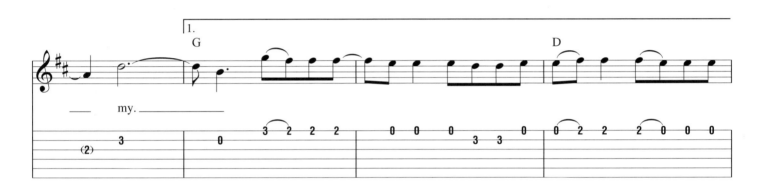

___ my. ___

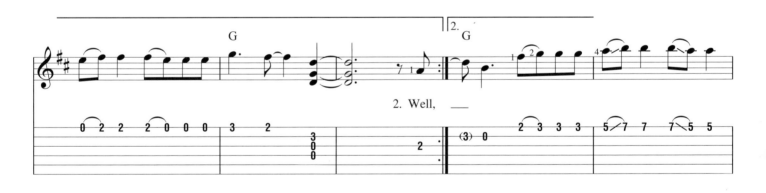

2. Well, ___

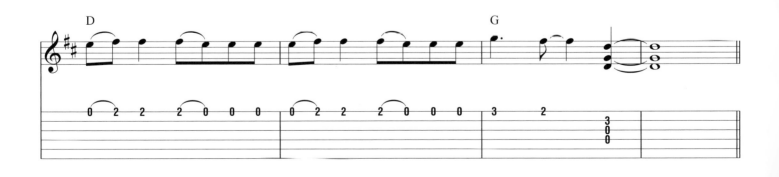

Bridge

A few years had gone and come a - round. __ We were sit - tin' at our fav'rite spot __ in town and you

D.S. al Coda

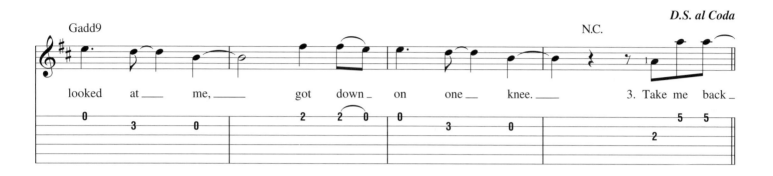

looked at __ me, ____ got down __ on one __ knee. ____ 3. Take me back __

⊕ Coda

And, I'll be eight-y - sev - en, you'll be eight-y - nine. __ I'll still look at you __ like the

*Let chords ring till end.

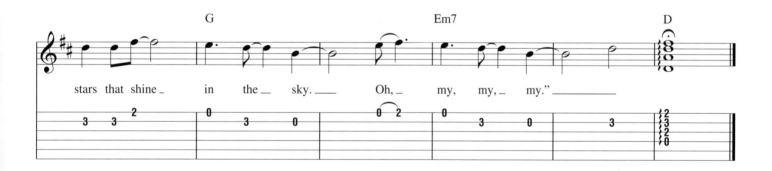

stars that shine __ in the __ sky. ____ Oh, __ my, my, __ my." _____

Additional Lyrics

2. Well, I was sixteen when suddenly
   I wasn't that little girl you used to see,
   But your eyes still shined like pretty lights.
   And our daddies used to joke about the two of us.
   They never believed we'd really fall in love.
   And our mamas smiled and rolled their eyes
   And said, 'Oh, my, my, my.'

Chorus 2. Take me back to the creek beds we turned up.
   Two A.M., ridin' in your truck, and all I need is you next to me.
   Take me back to the time we had our very first fight,
   The slammin' doors 'stead of kissin' goodnight.
   You stayed outside till the mornin' light.
   Oh, my, my, my, my.

Chorus 3. Take me back to the time when we walked down the aisle.
   Our whole town came and our mamas cried.
   You said, 'I do,' and I did, too.
   Take me home where we met so many years before.
   We'll rock our babies on that very front porch.
   After all this time, you and I.

Our Song

Words and Music by Taylor Swift

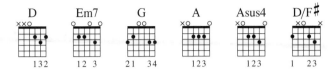

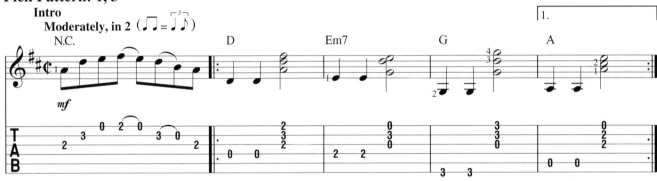

Strum Pattern: 2, 5
Pick Pattern: 1, 3

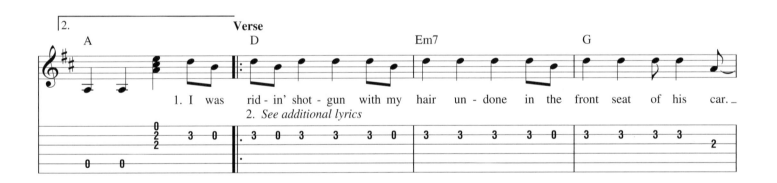

1. I was rid - in' shot - gun with my hair un - done in the front seat of his car.
2. See additional lyrics

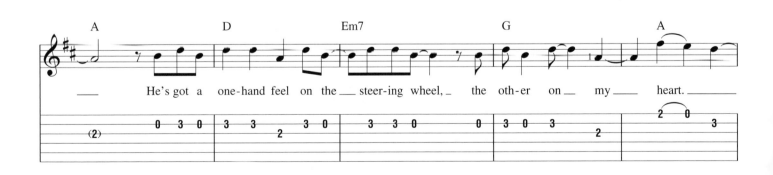

He's got a one-hand feel on the _ steer-ing wheel, _ the oth-er on _ my _ heart. _

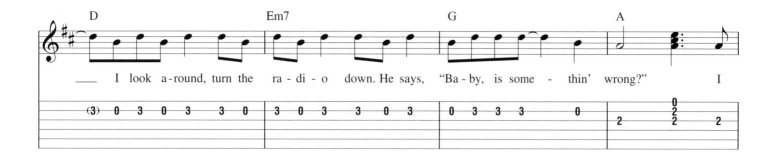

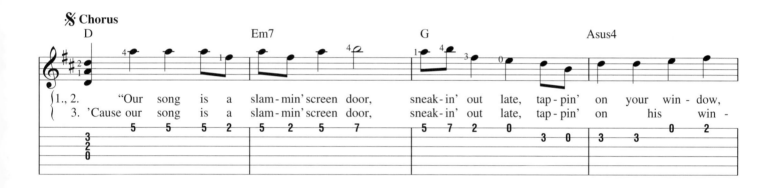

% Chorus

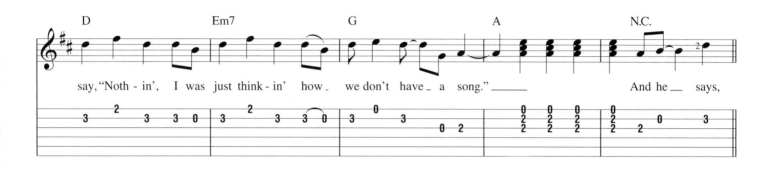

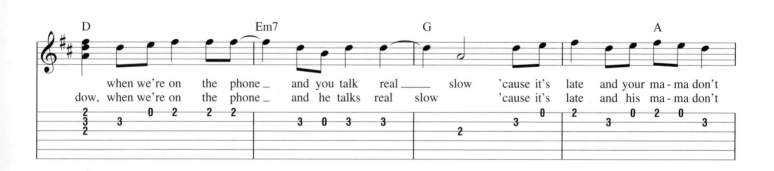

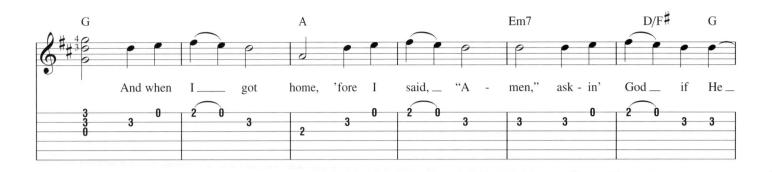

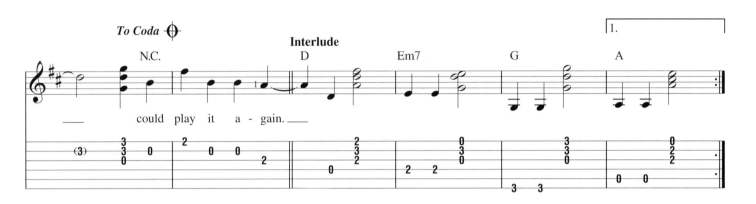

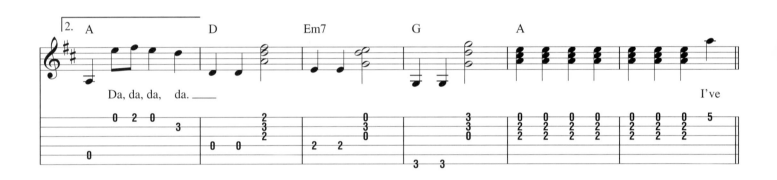

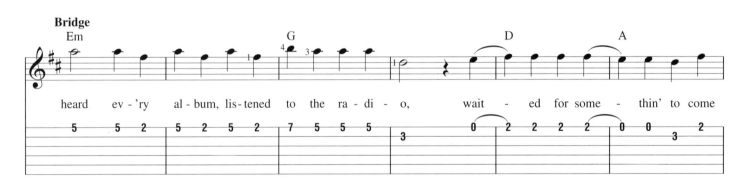

*Let chord ring.

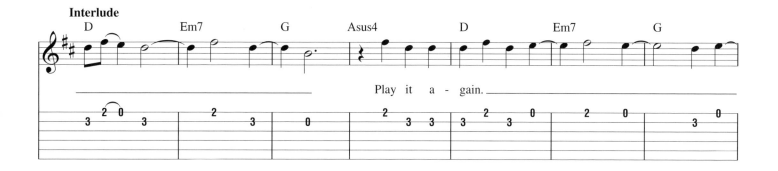

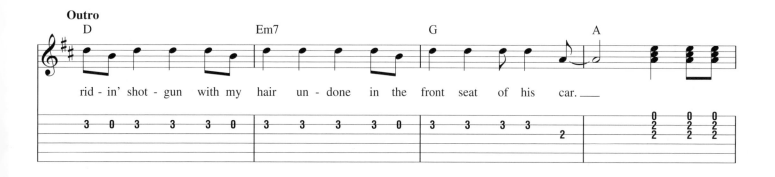

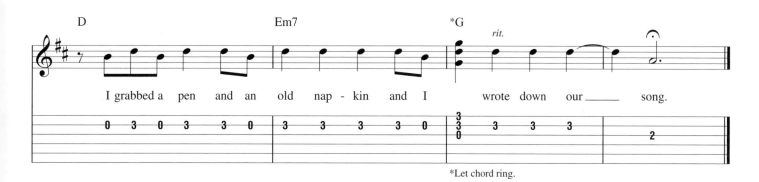

*Let chord ring.

Additional Lyrics

2. I was walkin' up the front porch steps after ev'rything that day
   Had gone all wrong, had been trampled on and lost and thrown away.
   Got to the hallway, well on my way to my lovin' bed.
   I almost didn't notice all the roses and the note that said...

Tied Together with a Smile

Words and Music by Taylor Swift and Liz Rose

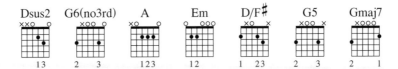

Strum Pattern: 3, 4
Pick Pattern: 1, 3

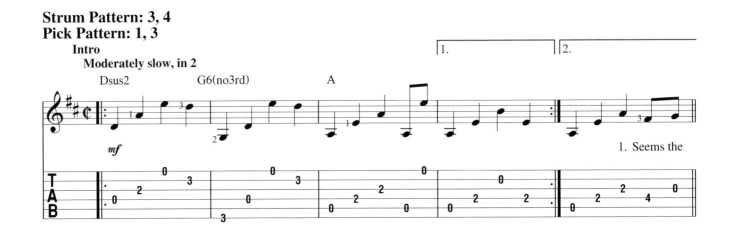

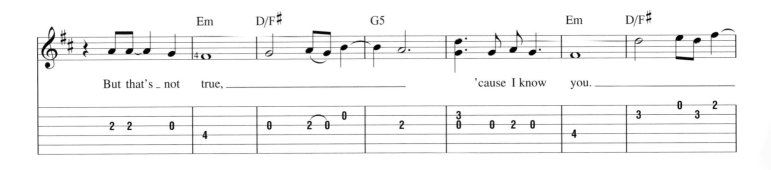

𝄋 Chorus

*3rd time, play chords in parentheses.

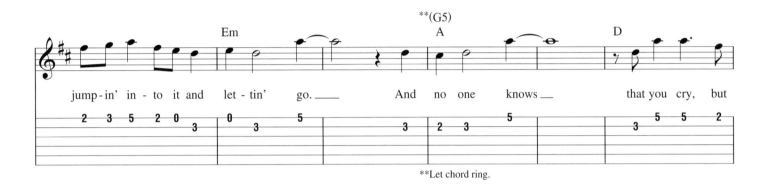

**Let chord ring.

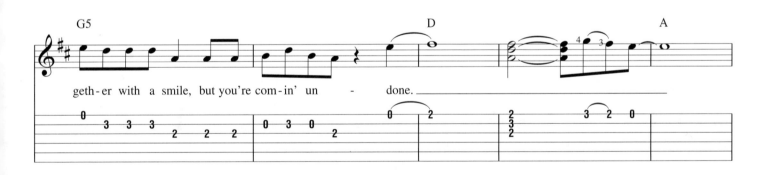

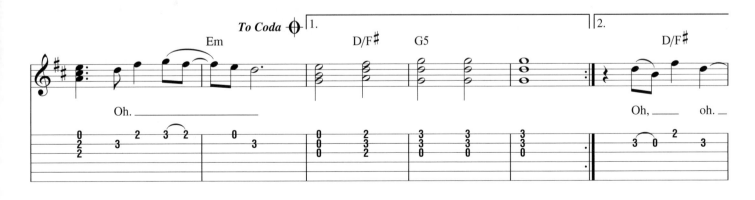

Coda

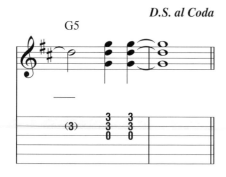

You're tied to - geth-er with a smile, but you're com-in' un - done. ___

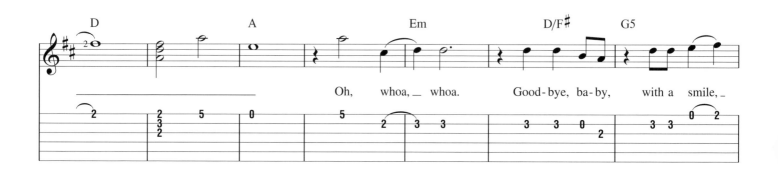

Oh, whoa, ___ whoa. Good - bye, ba - by, with a smile, ___

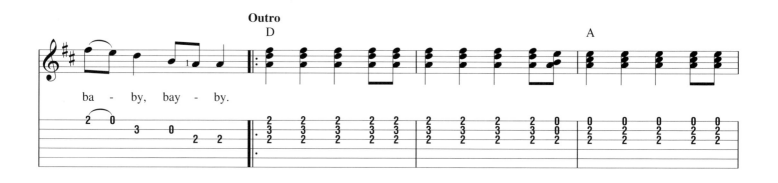

ba - by, bay - by.

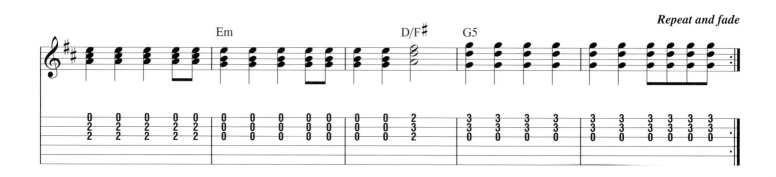

Additional Lyrics

2. I guess it's true that love was all you wanted
   'Cause you're givin' it away like it's extra change.
   Hopin' it will end up in his pocket.
   But he leaves you out like a penny in the rain,
   Oh, 'cause it's not his price to pay,
   It's not his price to pay.

EASY GUITAR
WITH NOTES & TAB

This series features simplified arrangements with notes, tab, chord charts, and strum and pick patterns.

MIXED FOLIOS	
00702002	Acoustic Rock Hits for Easy Guitar $12.95
00702166	All-Time Best Guitar Collection $17.95
00699665	Beatles Best $12.95
00702232	Best Acoustic Songs for Easy Guitar $12.99
00698978	Big Christmas Collection $16.95
00702115	Blues Classics $10.95
00385020	Broadway Songs for Kids $9.95
00702237	Christian Acoustic Favorites $12.95
00702149	Children's Christian Songbook $7.95
00702028	Christmas Classics $7.95
00702185	Christmas Hits $9.95
00702016	Classic Blues for Easy Guitar $12.95
00702141	Classic Rock $8.95
00702203	CMT's 100 Greatest Country Songs $27.95
00702170	Contemporary Christian Christmas $9.95
00702006	Contemporary Christian Favorites $9.95
00702065	Contemporary Women of Country $9.95
00702121	Country from the Heart $9.95
00702240	Country Hits of 2007-2008 ....$12.95
00702225	Country Hits of '06-'07 ....$12.95
00702085	Disney Movie Hits $12.95
00702212	Essential Christmas $9.95
00702041	Favorite Hymns for Easy Guitar $9.95
00702068	Forty Songs for a Better World $10.95
00702174	God Bless America® & Other Songs for a Better Nation $8.95
00699374	Gospel Favorites $14.95
00702160	The Great American Country Songbook $12.95
00702050	Great Classical Themes for Easy Guitar $6.95
00702131	Great Country Hits of the '90s $8.95
00702116	Greatest Hymns for Guitar $8.95
00702130	The Groovy Years $9.95
00702184	Guitar Instrumentals $9.95
00702231	High School Musical for Easy Guitar $12.95
00702241	High School Musical 2 ....$12.95
00702249	High School Musical 3 ....$12.99
00702037	Hits of the '50s for Easy Guitar $10.95
00702046	Hits of the '70s for Easy Guitar $8.95
00702047	Hits of the '80s for Easy Guitar $9.95
00702032	International Songs for Easy Guitar $12.95
00702051	Jock Rock for Easy Guitar $9.95
00702162	Jumbo Easy Guitar Songbook $19.95
00702112	Latin Favorites $9.95
00702138	Mellow Rock Hits $10.95
00702147	Motown's Greatest Hits $9.95
00702114	Movie Love Songs $9.95
00702039	Movie Themes $10.95
00702210	Best of MTV Unplugged $12.95
00702189	MTV's 100 Greatest Pop Songs $24.95
00702187	Selections from *O Brother Where Art Thou?* $12.95
00702178	100 Songs for Kids $12.95
00702158	Songs from Passion $9.95
00702125	Praise and Worship for Guitar $9.95
00702155	Rock Hits for Guitar $9.95
00702242	Rock Band $19.95
00702128	Rockin' Down the Highway $9.95
00702207	Smash Hits for Guitar $9.95
00702110	The Sound of Music $8.95
00702124	Today's Christian Rock – 2nd Edition $9.95
00702220	Today's Country Hits $9.95
00702198	Today's Hits for Guitar $9.95
00702217	Top Christian Hits $12.95
00702235	Top Christian Hits of '07-'08 ....$14.95
00702246	Top Hits of 2008 ....$12.95
00702206	Very Best of Rock $9.95
00702175	VH1's 100 Greatest Songs of Rock and Roll $24.95
00702192	Worship Favorites $9.95

ARTIST COLLECTIONS	
00702001	Best of Aerosmith $16.95
00702040	Best of the Allman Brothers $12.95
00702169	Best of The Beach Boys $10.95
00702201	The Essential Black Sabbath $12.95
00702140	Best of Brooks & Dunn $10.95
00702095	Best of Mariah Carey $12.95
00702043	Best of Johnny Cash $12.95
00702033	Best of Steven Curtis Chapman $14.95
00702073	Steven Curtis Chapman – Favorites $10.95
00702090	Eric Clapton's Best $10.95
00702086	Eric Clapton – from the Album *Unplugged* $10.95
00702202	The Essential Eric Clapton $12.95
00702053	Best of Patsy Cline $10.95
00702229	The Very Best of Creedence Clearwater Revival $12.95
00702145	Best of Jim Croce $10.95
00702219	David Crowder*Band Collection $12.95
00702122	The Doors for Easy Guitar $10.95
00702159	Best of Genesis $10.95
00702099	Best of Amy Grant $9.95
00702190	Best of Pat Green $19.95
00702136	Best of Merle Haggard $10.95
00702243	Hannah Montana $14.95
00702244	Hannah Montana 2/Meet Miley Cyrus $16.95
00702227	Jimi Hendrix – Smash Hits $12.95
00702236	Best of Antonio Carlos Jobim $12.95
00702087	Best of Billy Joel $10.95
00702088	Best of Elton John $9.95
00702204	Robert Johnson $9.95
00702199	Norah Jones – Come Away with Me $10.95
00702234	Selections from Toby Keith – 35 Biggest Hits $12.95
00702003	Kiss $9.95
00702193	Best of Jennifer Knapp $12.95
00702097	John Lennon – Imagine $9.95
00702216	Lynyrd Skynyrd $14.95
00702182	The Essential Bob Marley $12.95
00702129	Songs of Sarah McLachlan $12.95
00702209	Steve Miller Band – Young Hearts (Greatest Hits) ...$12.95
00702096	Best of Nirvana $14.95
00702211	The Offspring – Greatest Hits $12.95
00702030	Best of Roy Orbison $12.95
00702144	Best of Ozzy Osbourne $12.95
00702139	Elvis Country Favorites $9.95
00699415	Best of Queen for Guitar $12.95
00702208	Red Hot Chili Peppers – Greatest Hits $12.95
00702093	Rolling Stones Collection $17.95
00702092	Best of the Rolling Stones $12.95
00702196	Best of Bob Seger $12.95
00702010	Best of Rod Stewart $14.95
00702150	Best of Sting $12.95
00702049	Best of George Strait $12.95
00702223	Chris Tomlin – Arriving $12.95
00702226	Chris Tomlin – See the Morning $12.95
00702132	Shania Twain – Greatest Hits $10.95
00702108	Best of Stevie Ray Vaughan $10.95
00702123	Best of Hank Williams $9.95
00702111	Stevie Wonder – Guitar Collection $9.95
00702228	Neil Young – Greatest Hits $12.99
00702188	Essential ZZ Top $10.95

Prices, contents and availability subject to change without notice.

0109

HAL•LEONARD GUITAR PLAY-ALONG®

This series will help you play your favorite songs quickly and easily. **INCLUDES TAB**
Just follow the tab and listen to the CD to hear how the guitar should sound, and then play along using the separate backing tracks. Mac or PC users can also slow down the tempo without changing pitch by using the CD in their computer. The melody and lyrics are included in the book so that you can sing or simply follow along.

VOL. 1 – ROCK	00699570 / $16.99	
VOL. 2 – ACOUSTIC	00699569 / $16.95	
VOL. 3 – HARD ROCK	00699573 / $16.95	
VOL. 4 – POP/ROCK	00699571 / $16.99	
VOL. 5 – MODERN ROCK	00699574 / $16.99	
VOL. 6 – '90s ROCK	00699572 / $16.99	
VOL. 7 – BLUES	00699575 / $16.95	
VOL. 8 – ROCK	00699585 / $14.95	
VOL. 9 – PUNK ROCK	00699576 / $14.95	
VOL. 10 – ACOUSTIC	00699586 / $16.95	
VOL. 11 – EARLY ROCK	00699579 / $14.95	
VOL. 12 – POP/ROCK	00699587 / $14.95	
VOL. 13 – FOLK ROCK	00699581 / $14.95	
VOL. 14 – BLUES ROCK	00699582 / $16.95	
VOL. 15 – R&B	00699583 / $14.95	
VOL. 16 – JAZZ	00699584 / $15.95	
VOL. 17 – COUNTRY	00699588 / $15.95	
VOL. 18 – ACOUSTIC ROCK	00699577 / $15.95	
VOL. 19 – SOUL	00699578 / $14.95	
VOL. 20 – ROCKABILLY	00699580 / $14.95	
VOL. 21 – YULETIDE	00699602 / $14.95	
VOL. 22 – CHRISTMAS	00699600 / $15.95	
VOL. 23 – SURF	00699635 / $14.95	
VOL. 24 – ERIC CLAPTON	00699649 / $16.95	
VOL. 25 – LENNON & McCARTNEY	00699642 / $14.95	
VOL. 26 – ELVIS PRESLEY	00699643 / $14.95	
VOL. 27 – DAVID LEE ROTH	00699645 / $16.95	
VOL. 28 – GREG KOCH	00699646 / $14.95	
VOL. 29 – BOB SEGER	00699647 / $14.95	
VOL. 30 – KISS	00699644 / $14.95	
VOL. 31 – CHRISTMAS HITS	00699652 / $14.95	
VOL. 32 – THE OFFSPRING	00699653 / $14.95	
VOL. 33 – ACOUSTIC CLASSICS	00699656 / $16.95	
VOL. 34 – CLASSIC ROCK	00699658 / $16.95	
VOL. 35 – HAIR METAL	00699660 / $16.95	
VOL. 36 – SOUTHERN ROCK	00699661 / $16.95	
VOL. 37 – ACOUSTIC METAL	00699662 / $16.95	
VOL. 38 – BLUES	00699663 / $16.95	
VOL. 39 – '80s METAL	00699664 / $16.99	
VOL. 40 – INCUBUS	00699668 / $17.95	
VOL. 41 – ERIC CLAPTON	00699669 / $16.95	
VOL. 42 – CHART HITS	00699670 / $16.95	
VOL. 43 – LYNYRD SKYNYRD	00699681 / $17.95	
VOL. 44 – JAZZ	00699689 / $14.95	
VOL. 45 – TV THEMES	00699718 / $14.95	
VOL. 46 – MAINSTREAM ROCK	00699722 / $16.95	
VOL. 47 – HENDRIX SMASH HITS	00699723 / $19.95	
VOL. 48 – AEROSMITH CLASSICS	00699724 / $16.99	
VOL. 49 – STEVIE RAY VAUGHAN	00699725 / $16.95	
VOL. 50 – NÜ METAL	00699726 / $14.95	
VOL. 51 – ALTERNATIVE '90s	00699727 / $12.95	
VOL. 52 – FUNK	00699728 / $14.95	
VOL. 53 – DISCO	00699729 / $12.99	
VOL. 54 – HEAVY METAL	00699730 / $14.95	
VOL. 55 – POP METAL	00699731 / $14.95	
VOL. 56 – FOO FIGHTERS	00699749 / $14.95	
VOL. 57 – SYSTEM OF A DOWN	00699751 / $14.95	
VOL. 58 – BLINK-182	00699772 / $14.95	
VOL. 59 – GODSMACK	00699773 / $14.95	
VOL. 60 – 3 DOORS DOWN	00699774 / $14.95	
VOL. 61 – SLIPKNOT	00699775 / $14.95	
VOL. 62 – CHRISTMAS CAROLS	00699798 / $12.95	
VOL. 63 – CREEDENCE CLEARWATER REVIVAL	00699802 / $16.99	
VOL. 64 – THE ULTIMATE OZZY OSBOURNE	00699803 / $16.99	
VOL. 65 – THE DOORS	00699806 / $16.99	
VOL. 66 – THE ROLLING STONES	00699807 / $16.95	
VOL. 67 – BLACK SABBATH	00699808 / $16.99	
VOL. 68 – PINK FLOYD – DARK SIDE OF THE MOON	00699809 / $16.99	
VOL. 69 – ACOUSTIC FAVORITES	00699810 / $14.95	
VOL. 70 – OZZY OSBOURNE	00699805 / $14.95	
VOL. 71 – CHRISTIAN ROCK	00699824 / $14.95	
VOL. 72 – ACOUSTIC '90S	00699827 / $14.95	
VOL. 74 – PAUL BALOCHE	00699831 / $14.95	
VOL. 75 – TOM PETTY	00699882 / $16.99	
VOL. 76 – COUNTRY HITS	00699884 / $14.95	
VOL. 78 – NIRVANA	00700132 / $14.95	
VOL. 80 – ACOUSTIC ANTHOLOGY	00700175 / $19.95	
VOL. 81 – ROCK ANTHOLOGY	00700176 / $22.99	
VOL. 82 – EASY SONGS	00700177 / $12.99	
VOL. 83 – THREE CHORD SONGS	00700178 / $12.99	
VOL. 96 – THIRD DAY	00700560 / $14.95	
VOL. 97 – ROCK BAND	00700703 / $14.99	
VOL. 98 – ROCK BAND	00700704 / $14.95	

Prices, contents, and availability subject to change without notice.

FOR MORE INFORMATION, SEE YOUR LOCAL MUSIC DEALER, OR WRITE TO:

7777 W. BLUEMOUND RD. P.O. BOX 13819 MILWAUKEE, WI 53213

Visit Hal Leonard online at www.halleonard.com

Complete song lists available online.

0309